T0151603

# Incredible Jello

Naomi Hakamata

## Preface

Sweetness is not the only enjoyable quality of jello, you
can also enjoy its mature flavor. Such thoughts were
the impetus for beginning this project. This book offers
recipes that can be enjoyed on a variety of occasions,
from teatime desserts to appetizers that will complement
any dinner party champagne or wine. The recipes do
not require the use of a mold because they use the fruit
and vegetable peels themselves as molds. This allows us
to savor the aroma of those fruits and vegetables again.
Also, using freshly squeezed juice makes for healthier
jello that are loaded with vitamins. Such jello are eye-
pleasing delights that offer up the pleasant aroma of
nature. As a bonus, they can be made quickly and easily,
and do not require any difficult-to-use utensils. In order
to enjoy many different types of jello throughout the
year, the recipes presented here use seasonal ingredients.
Please enjoy all of these mature, flavor-filled jello.
I sincerely hope these recipes bring smiles to you and all
those you love and care about.

Naomi Hakamata

Table of Contents

## APPETIZERS

This book was created in Japan and the recipes were developed using Japanese measurement, which means that the ingredients were measured in g and ml. The recipes were converted into US measurements to the best of the publisher's ability. However, it is possible that minute discrepancies have occurred between the original recipes and the converted recipes. Moreover, the juiciness and size of the fruits and vegetables available in your area will vary. That being said, please feel free to make fine adjustments to the recipes presented here, especially when it comes to the amount of gelling agent. As a matter of fact, it is important to always read the directions provided (usually printed on the package) before using gelling agents and then make adjustment to the recipes as necessary.

| **Regarding Recipes** |

- 1 teaspoon = 5ml

- 1 tablespoon = 15ml

- 1 cup = 240 ml

- When a very small amount of seasoning or spice is required for a recipe, it is described as either "a little" or "a pinch."

- "A little" is about the amount pinched between your thumb and middle finger. "A pinch" is about an amount pinched with thumb, index, and middle finger.

- "As desired" refers to the correct amount to satisfy the chef's palette, and "optional" simply means that adding the ingredient is optional.

## Ingredients

This book presents recipes for jello that use easy-to-find, seasonal, fruits and vegetables.

• Sweetener
Recipes use minimal amounts of sweetener to allow for the greatest enjoyment of each fruit's natural sweetness. Granulated sugar, which brings out the transparency of the jello, is the most used sweetener but recipes also use coconut syrup, gum syrup, honey, or condensed milk to achieve certain effects.

• Flavoring
Adding alcohol, such as wine or liqueur, enhances aroma and produces a mature flavor. Those who are not fond of alcohol, or who wish to enjoy their creations with children, can just substitute a soda or juice of their choice. If you do not enjoy drinking regularly, it is not necessary to purchase a large bottle of liqueur, just purchase a mini bottle instead.

• Sourness
Adding a small amount of sourness, like wine vinegar or balsamic vinegar, enhances the freshness of the jello. Similarly, adding lemon juice will prevent oxidization of fruits that are prone to discoloration.

• Agar

The recipes in this book mostly use agar as a gelling agent. Agar is made from algae or an extract from legume-family plant seeds. Agar will set up transparent and smooth, and produce a soft, plump texture. It is tasteless and flavorless so you can fully enjoy the aroma and taste of your chosen fruits and vegetables. Agar is easy to handle as well because it easily stands up to room temperature. However, make sure it is properly dissolved in a liquid prior to heating as it tends to clump. If you prefer soft jello, use about ¼ tablespoon (2 g) less agar than the recipe requires. That way you can enjoy lightly textured jello.

• Gelatin

Gelatin is made from animal collagen. The recipes in this book use two different forms of gelatin, powdered and leaf. Gelatin produces elastic, soft, plump textures that melt in the mouth. However, gelatin does not stand up well to room temperature and easily deforms, so it is best to consume jello made from gelatin soon after removing them from the refrigerator. Especially in summer.

• *Kanten* (Japanese agar)

Made from red algae and *Gracilaria, kanten* produces a soft and "fun-to-bite-into" texture that offers a unique and pleasant taste which is different from agar and gelatin. *Kanten* does not dissolve readily in liquid, so be sure to cook it for a couple of minutes after reaching its boiling point. Cook until the *kanten* has completely melted and the remaining liquid becomes translucent.

# Utensils

The recipes in this book use fruits and vegetables as molds.
This section introduces utensils that are helpful for creating and manipulating such molds.

• To Cut
Since the recipes use fruit and vegetable peels as molds, it is best to use a sharp knife that will create finely cut angles. This will enhance the final results.

• To Remove Flesh
A grapefruit knife and a melon-baller will come in handy when scooping out fruit flesh. However, If you don't have a grapefruit knife, you can just use a paring knife. Also, a melon-baller can easily be substituted with a measuring spoon.

• To Juice
Use a lemon squeezer to juice citrus fruits. If that is not an option, just use your hands. But, be sure to only use the juice after you have filtered out the seeds with a sieve.

• To Measure
Use measuring spoons, measuring cups, or a scale to prepare ingredients called for in the recipe. A measuring cup comes in handy for pouring gelatin/agar mixtures into fruit peel molds.

• To Stabilize Fruit Peel Molds
Stabilizing the hollowed fruit and vegetable molds is important for preventing spillage of the gelatin/agar mixture. Muffin tins or baking sheets lined with wrinkled plastic wrap or aluminum foil are used to stabilize molds throughout this book. An airtight container (plastic) can be used if a muffin tin or baking sheet is not available. Regardless of what you use, stabilizing the molds is very important.

• To Mix
A small saucepan works fine for dissolving agar or gelatin into a liquid. A whisk is very convenient for combining mixtures. If a whisk is not available, you can use a spatula instead.

• To Enhance the Finished Look
When agar is added to a liquid occasionally impurities or bubbles will form (especially with citrus juices). Having said that, it is recommended that you filter the agar mixture with a sieve in order to make sure the gelled surface turns out beautiful.

# | DESSERTS |

The juice and aroma of each fruit flows out when cut.
Gelatin desserts introduced in this section capture the
deliciousness and freshness of each fruit. Throughout
the year you can enjoy recipes and savor all of the in
season fruits.

# Strawberry Almond Tofu Jello

## Ingredients

(Makes twenty strawberry jello cups)

- 20 strawberries (medium sized)
- $1/3$ cup plus 4 teaspoons (100 ml) water
- $1/3$ cup plus 4 teaspoons (100 ml) milk
- $1/4$ cup (60 ml) heavy cream
- 5 tablespoons (30 g) almond powder
- 3 tablespoons plus 1 teaspoon (40 g) granulated sugar
- 2 teaspoons (6 g) agar
- 2 tablespoons amaretto
  (or a few drops of almond extract)

## Preparation

Trim off strawberry stems. For each strawberry, hollow out the top half of the flesh using a spoon or small melon-baller (see photo A).

## Instructions

1 Prepare strips of aluminum foil. Fold each strip into a wave-like shape. Place the folded strips on the baking sheet to make indentations that will hold the strawberries. Place each strawberry in an upright position (stem side up) on the baking sheet.

2 Combine granulated sugar and agar in a small bowl.

3 Add water and almond powder to a small saucepan. Gradually, add the sugar and agar mixture to the saucepan and whisk until dissolved.

4 Bring to a boil over medium heat. Once boiling, remove from heat. Then, add milk and heavy cream. Stir well. Again, heat on medium. Remove saucepan from the heat just before it boils.

5 Add amaretto. Pour mixture into a measuring cup, using a sieve, and allow to cool.

6 Once the mixture is cool enough to handle, fill each hollowed out strawberry (see photo B). Once the top of the jello has set, refrigerate for about an hour.

7 Transfer the strawberry jello to a dish. Sprinkle on some granulated sugar (not included in the recipe) and serve.

## TIPS

Be sure to place each strawberry securely on the baking sheet so they don't tip over as the jello is poured in from the stem side.

# Mangosteen Coconut Cream Jello

## Ingredients

(Makes twelve mangosteen shell jello cups)

- 12 mangosteens, whole flesh
- ³⁄₄ cup plus 4 teaspoons (200 ml) coconut cream
- ³⁄₄ cup plus 4 teaspoons (200 ml) milk
- ¹⁄₃ cup plus 5 teaspoons (80 g) granulated sugar
- 2 tablespoons lemon juice
- 6 g leaf gelatin
- 2 tablespoons chia seeds
- 2 teaspoons coconut syrup

## Preparation

Trim around mangosteen stems to remove a round shaped piece of flesh (see photo A). Save the stems. Then, remove the remaining flesh (see photo B).

Cut the flesh in half and sprinkle on some lemon juice to prevent oxidization. Refrigerate half of the flesh and the stems.

Soak gelatin leaves in cold water and soak chia seeds in 4 tablespoons of water (not included in the recipe) to soften.

## Instructions

1 Wrinkle up some plastic wrap and lay it on a baking sheet. Then, place each hollowed mangosteen on the sheet.

2 Add the coconut cream, milk, and granulated sugar to a small saucepan and heat on medium. Remove the saucepan just before it boils. Remove moisture from the gelatin then add to the saucepan and whisk well to dissolve.

3 Put the bottom of the saucepan in a bowl filled with ice water to cool.

4 Once the mixture is cool enough to handle, add the coconut syrup and soaked chia seeds. Stir well.

5 Put the non-refrigerated mangosteen flesh inside of each hollowed out mangosteen.

6 Fill each mangosteen with the gelatin mixture. Refrigerate for about an hour to set.

7 Once the jello has set, put the refrigerated flesh on top of each mangosteen jello. Then, place stems on top.

# Lychee Coconut Water Jello

## Ingredients

(Makes forty lychee shell jello cups)

- 40 lychees, whole flesh
- $1^2/_3$ cups (400 ml) coconut water
- 2 tablespoons plus $1^1/_2$ teaspoons (30 g) granulated sugar
- 4 teaspoons (12 g) agar
- 2 tablespoons lychee liqueur (optional)

## Preparation

Trim off $^1/_3$ of the lychee skin (see photo). Remove the flesh. Remove pit and coarsely dice the flesh.

## Instructions

1 Wrinkle up plastic wrap and then lay it on a baking sheet. Then, securely place each hollowed lychee on the sheet.

2 Put the diced flesh inside each hollowed lychee.

3 Combine granulated sugar and agar in a small bowl.

4 Add coconut water to a small saucepan. Gradually, add the sugar and agar mixture to the saucepan and whisk until dissolved.

5 Bring to a boil over medium heat. Once boiling, remove from heat. Add lychee liqueur to the mixture. Pour mixture through a sieve into a measuring cup. Allow to cool.

6 Once the mixture is cool enough to handle, fill each hollowed lychee. Once the top of the jello has set, refrigerate for an hour.

# Grapefruit Jello

## Ingredients

(Makes eight halved grapefruit shell jello cups)

- 4 pink and 4 white grapefruits
- 24 raspberries (frozen)
- Sea salt as desired

\<Pink Grapefruit Jello\>
- 1²/₃ cups (400 ml) pink grapefruit juice
- ³/₄ cup (180 g) pink grapefruit flesh
- ¹/₃ cup (60 g) granulated sugar
- 2 tablespoons (16 g) agar
- 2 tablespoons Grand Marnier (optional)

\<White Grapefruit Jello\>
- 2¹/₂ cups (600 ml) white grapefruit juice
- ¹/₃ cup plus 2¹/₂ tablespoons (90 g) granulated sugar
- 3 tablespoons (24 g) agar
- 4 tablespoons tequila (substitute with juice if desired)
- 1 tablespoon Grand Marnier (optional)

## TIPS

The recipe uses frozen raspberries, but they can be substituted with the fruit of your choice.

## Preparation

Use two pink grapefruits to prepare the juice called for in the recipe. Peel the remaining two grapefruits and score along the inner membrane to remove the flesh. Set aside the flesh called for in the recipe.

Halve all four white grapefruits. Use a grapefruit knife to remove the flesh (see photo) and then remove remaining membrane. Squeeze flesh to prepare the juice called for in the recipe.

## Instructions

1 Stabilize all eight white grapefruit halves in a muffin tin or a bowl that fits the halves tightly.

2 Crumble frozen raspberries and put them inside of each grapefruit half.

3 Prepare pink grapefruit jello. Combine granulated sugar and agar in a small bowl. Pour juice into a small saucepan. Add the sugar and agar mixture gradually to the saucepan and whisk until dissolved. Bring to a boil over medium heat. Once boiling, remove from heat. Then, add bite-sized flesh and Grand Marnier to the saucepan. Stir well. Once the mixture is cool enough to handle, quickly pour it into each grapefruit half using a ladle. Once the top of the jello has set, refrigerate for about twenty minutes.

4 Prepare white grapefruit jello. Combine granulated sugar and agar in a small bowl. Pour half of the juice into a small saucepan. Gradually, add the sugar and agar mixture to the saucepan and whisk until dissolved. Bring to a boil over medium heat. Once boiling, remove from heat. Then, add the remaining juice, tequila, and Grand Marnier. Stir well. Heat the saucepan again to bring to a boil. Once boiling, remove from heat. Pour mixture through a sieve into a measuring cup. Allow to cool. Once the mixture is cool enough to handle, take out the pink grapefruit jello from the refrigerator. Then, pour enough white grapefruit jello mixture to fill each half of the grapefruit.

5 Once the top of the jello has set, refrigerate for about an hour to set.

6 Cut as desired and serve with sea salt.

### TIPS
Feel free to use the leftover lemon flesh and juice to make a salad or some salad dressing. After you have poured the blue curaçao flavored mixture into each lemon, keep them at room temperature. Then, pour the lemon flavored mixture in such a way that it creates gradations of the two colors in each lemon shell.

# Lemon Jello

## Ingredients
(Makes eight halved lemon shell jello cups)

- 4 lemons
- 6 tablespoons lemon juice
- ¾ cup (180 ml) water

## Preparation
Halve each lemon lengthwise. Remove the flesh and set aside to juice. Remove all remaining inner membranes.

Squeeze the flesh for the juice required by the recipe.

## Instructions
1 Place the hollowed lemons in a muffin tin or a baking sheet lined with wrinkled plastic wrap.

2 Combine granulated sugar and agar in a small bowl.

- 3 tablespoons plus 1 teaspoon (40 g) granulated sugar
- 4 teaspoons (12 g) agar
- 4 tablespoons limoncello

(substitute with lemon juice if desired)

3 Pour the lemon juice and water into a small saucepan. Add the sugar and agar mixture and whisk until dissolved.

4 Bring to a boil over medium heat. Once boiling, remove from heat. Then, add limoncello and stir well.

5 Pour mixture into a measuring cup over a sieve and let cool. Once it is cool enough to handle, pour into each hollowed lemon. Fill to the edge.

6 Once the top of the jello has set, refrigerate for an hour or so. Cut as desired and serve.

# Limoncello Blue Curaçao Jello

## Ingredients
(Makes sixteen halved lemon shell Jello cups)

- 8 lemons

<Blue Curaçao Jello>
- ¾ cup plus 4 teaspoons (200 ml) water
- 4 tablespoons blue curaçao
- ⅓ cup (60 g) granulated sugar
- 4 teaspoons (12 g) agar

## Preparation
Halve each lemon lengthwise. Remove the flesh and set aside to juice. Remove all remaining inner membranes.

Squeeze the flesh for the juice required by the recipe.

## Instructions
1 Place the hollowed lemons in a muffin tin or a baking sheet lined with wrinkled plastic wrap.

2 Prepare blue curaçao jello. Combine granulated sugar and agar in a small bowl. Pour water into a small saucepan then gradually add the sugar and agar mixture. Whisk until dissolved. Bring to a boil over medium heat. Once boiling, remove from heat. Then, add blue curaçao and stir well. Transfer the

<Lemon Jello>
- 6 tablespoons lemon juice
- ¾ cup (180 ml) water
- 3 tablespoons plus 1 teaspoon (40 g) granulated sugar
- 4 teaspoons (12 g) agar
- 2 tablespoons limoncello

mixture to a measuring cup and let cool. Once the mixture is cool enough to handle, pour it into the hollowed lemons. Fill to the halfway point. Set aside and leave at room temperature.

3 Prepare lemon jello. Combine granulated sugar and agar in a small bowl. Pour lemon juice and water into a small saucepan. Gradually, add the sugar and agar mixture to the saucepan and whisk until dissolved. Bring to a boil over medium heat. Once boiling, remove from heat. Then, add limoncello and stir well. Pour mixture into a measuring cup through a sieve and let cool. Once the mixture is cool enough to handle, pour it into the half-filled lemon shells. Fill up to the edge. Once the top of the jello has set, refrigerate for an hour or so. Cut as desired and serve.

# Lime Guava Jello

## Ingredients
(Makes twelve halved lime shell jello cups)

- 6 limes
- 4 tablespoons lime juice
- $1^2/3$ cups (400 ml) guava juice
- 3 tablespoons plus 1 teaspoon (40 g) granulated sugar
- $2^1/2$ tablespoons (20 g) agar
- 4 tablespoons white rum (substitute with guava juice if desired)
- Fresh mint leaves as desired

## Preparation
Halve each lime lengthwise. Remove the flesh and set aside to juice. Remove all remaining inner membranes.

Squeeze the flesh for the juice required by the recipe.

## Instructions

1 Place the hollowed limes in a muffin tin or a baking sheet lined with wrinkled plastic wrap.

2 Combine granulated sugar and agar in a small bowl.

3 Pour lime and guava juice into a small saucepan. Gradually, add the sugar and agar mixture and whisk until dissolved.

4 Bring to a boil over medium heat. Once boiling, remove from heat. Then, add the white rum and stir.

5 Pour mixture into a measuring cup through a sieve and let cool. Once the mixture is cool enough to handle, pour into the lime shells. Fill to the edge. Once the top of the jello has set, refrigerate for an hour or so.

6 Cut as desired and garnish with the fresh mint leaves to serve.

**TIPS**
Feel free to use the remaining lime flesh and juice as you wish. For example, you can make a salad or salad dressing.

# Two-Color Orange Jello

## Ingredients

(Makes eight halved orange shell jello cups)

• 6 oranges

[A: Dark Color]
• 1$\frac{2}{3}$ cups (400 ml) blood orange juice
  (use no sugar added juice,
  not from concentrate)
• $\frac{1}{3}$ cup (60 g) granulated sugar
• 6 teaspoons (18 g) agar
• 2 tablespoons Cointreau (optional)

[B: Light Color]
• 2 cups plus 1$\frac{1}{3}$ tablespoons (500 ml)
  orange juice
• $\frac{1}{3}$ cup (60 g) granulated sugar
• 2$\frac{1}{2}$ tablespoons (20 g) agar
• 2 tablespoons Cointreau (optional)

## Preparation

Halve each orange lengthwise. Remove the flesh from eight halved oranges and set aside. Remove remaining inner membranes as well.

Use the remaining halved oranges and the removed flesh to prepare the orange juice called for in the recipe.

## Instructions

1 Place the hollowed oranges on a muffin tin or a baking sheet lined with wrinkled plastic wrap.

2 Prepare [A]. Combine granulated sugar and agar in a small bowl. Pour half of the blood orange juice into a small saucepan. Gradually, add the sugar and agar mixture to the saucepan and whisk until dissolved. Bring to a boil over medium heat. Once boiling, add the remaining blood orange juice and stir. Bring to a boil again. Then, remove saucepan from heat. Add the Cointreau and stir. Transfer the mixture to a measuring cup and let cool. Once cool enough to handle, pour the mixture into the hollowed oranges. Fill halfway.

3 Prepare [B]. Combine granulated sugar and agar in a small bowl. Pour half of the juice into a small saucepan. Gradually add the sugar and agar mixture to the saucepan and whisk until dissolved. Bring to a boil over medium heat. Once boiling, add the remaining juice and stir. Bring to a boil again. Then, remove saucepan from heat. Add the Cointreau and stir. Pour mixture into a measuring cup through a sieve and let cool. Once the mixture is cool enough to handle, pour into each half-filled orange until full. Once the top of the jello has set, refrigerate for an hour.

## TIPS

After you have poured mixture [A] into each orange shell, keep at room temperature. Then, add mixture [B] to create gradations of the two colors in each orange shell.

Layered Melon Jello p.28

Frozen Peach Jello p. 29

## Ingredients

(Makes four halved melon shell jello cups)

- 2 melons (either green or red flesh)

&lt;Coconut Jello&gt;
- $2/3$ cup (160 ml) coconut cream
- 2 tablespoons plus 2 teaspoons (40 ml) milk
- 2 tablespoons condensed milk
- 1 tablespoon (8 g) agar

&lt;Melon Jello&gt;
- $1^2/3$ cups (400 ml) juice
- $1/3$ cup plus 4 teaspoons (100 ml) water
- 2 tablespoons white wine (can be substituted with soda)
- $1/3$ cup (60 g) granulated sugar
- $3^1/2$ tablespoons (28 g) agar

&lt;White Wine Jello&gt;
- $3/4$ cup plus 4 teaspoons (200 ml) white wine (can be substituted with soda)
- $3/4$ cup plus 4 teaspoons (200 ml) water
- 2 tablespoons lemon juice
- 3 tablespoons plus 1 teaspoon (40 g) granulated sugar
- $2^1/2$ tablespoons (20 g) agar

# Layered Melon Jello

## Preparation

Halve each melon lengthwise and remove seeds. Score a line $1/2$" (1 cm) in from the skin using a grapefruit knife. Use a spoon or melon-baller to scoop out the flesh along the scored line and set aside. Juice the flesh to prepare the juice called for in the recipe.

## Instructions

1  Secure each halved melon in a snug-fitting bowl, and tilt at an angle.

2  Prepare coconut jello. Combine all of the ingredients in a small saucepan. Bring to a boil over medium heat while stirring. Once boiling, remove saucepan from heat. Pour mixture through a sieve into a measuring cup. Allow to cool. Once the mixture is cool enough to handle, pour it in each halved melon shell secured at an angle in a bowl. Once the top of the jello has set, refrigerate for about twenty minutes.

3  Prepare melon jello. Combine granulated sugar and agar in a small bowl. Pour water and white wine into a small saucepan. Gradually, add the sugar and agar mixture to the small saucepan and whisk until dissolved. Bring to a boil over medium heat. Then, add the juice and stir. Bring to a boil again. Once boiling, remove saucepan from heat. Pour the mixture into a measuring cup. Allow to cool. Remove melon shells from the refrigerator. Shift each melon shell so that it sits at less of an angle in the bowl and then pour in the mixture. Once the top of the jello has set, refrigerate for about twenty minutes again.

4  Prepare white wine jello. Combine granulated sugar and agar in a small bowl. Pour white wine and water into a small saucepan. Gradually, add the sugar and agar mixture to the saucepan and whisk until dissolved. Bring to a boil over medium heat. Once boiling, remove saucepan from heat. Pour mixture through a sieve into a measuring cup. Once the mixture is cool enough to handle, remove melon shells from refrigerator. Adjust each melon shell so that it sits flat in the bowl. Then, add mixture to fill each melon shell up to the edge.

5  Once the top of the jello has set, transfer melon shells to a baking sheet. Then, refrigerate for an hour. To serve, cut each melon shell as desired.

### TIPS

Secure each melon shell at an angle in a bowl. After each layer of jello poured, rearrange the melon shell so it sits at less of an angle. Pour the next mixture layer only after the previous layer has completely set. This makes for beautiful layers.

# Frozen Peach Jello

## Ingredients

(Makes four halved peach shell jello cups)

- 4 peaches
- Flesh of 2 peaches
- 4 tablespoons lemon juice
- $1\frac{1}{4}$ cups (300 ml) rose sparkling wine
  (can be substituted with soda)
- $1\frac{1}{4}$ cups (300 ml) water
- $\frac{1}{3}$ cup plus $2\frac{1}{2}$ tablespoons (90 g) granulated sugar
- 2 tablespoons plus 2 teaspoons (22 g) agar

\<Peach Puree\>

- 1 cup (200 g) peach flesh (pureed)
- 2 tablespoons lemon juice
- 2 tablespoons gum syrup
- 2 tablespoons peach liqueur (optional)

## Preparation

Slice through the peach until you feel the knife hit the pit. Slice completely around the peach and then, using your hands, gently twist each side of the peach in opposite directions and pull apart the two halves.

Take the half of the peach without the pit and use a grapefruit knife to score a line $\frac{1}{2}$" (1 cm) in from the skin. Scoop out the flesh along the scored line. Refrigerate the flesh for the peach puree required by the recipe.

Freeze the hollowed peach shells.

Peel the skin off and slice the half peaches with the pit. Transfer the peach slices to an airtight container and drizzle lemon juice on them to prevent oxidization. Then, refrigerate.

## Instructions

1  Combine granulated sugar and agar in a small bowl.

2  Pour rose sparkling wine and water into a small saucepan. Gradually, add the sugar and agar mixture and whisk until dissolved.

3  Bring to a boil over medium heat. Once boiling, remove saucepan from heat. Allow to cool.

4  Once the mixture is cool enough to handle, pour over the peach slices in the airtight container. Refrigerate for about an hour or so to set.

5  Add the peach puree ingredients to a food processor. Pulse to create peach puree.

6  Just before serving, break the peach jello into pieces and spoon into each frozen peach shell. Add a dollop of the peach puree on top and serve.

## TIPS

This frozen peach jello can be enjoyed without the peach puree. If you choose not to serve with peach puree, enjoy the scooped-out flesh as you wish.

# Watermelon Jello

## Ingredients

(Makes two halved mini-watermelon shell jello cups)

- 1 mini-watermelon [diameter $7^{1}/2$" (19 cm)]
- $1^{2}/3$ cups (400 ml) juice
- 2 cups plus $1^{1}/3$ tablespoons (500 ml) rose sparkling wine (can be substituted with soda)
- $^{1}/2$ cup plus 2 tablespoons (120 g) granulated sugar
- $4^{1}/2$ tablespoons (36 g) agar
- Sea salt as desired

## Preparation

Halve a mini-watermelon.

Use a grapefruit knife to score a line $1^{1}/4$" (3 cm) in from the skin. Scoop out the flesh using a spoon or melon-baller along the scored line.

Put the flesh in a sieve and mash using a spatula to prepare the juice called for in the recipe (see photo).

## Instructions

1 Secure each halved mini-watermelon in a snug-fitting bowl.

2 Combine granulated sugar and agar in a small bowl.

3 Pour rose sparkling wine into a small saucepan. Gradually, add the sugar and agar mixture and whisk until dissolved.

4 Bring to a boil over medium heat. Once boiling, add the juice and stir well. Bring to a boil again. And then, remove from heat.

5 Pour mixture through a sieve into a measuring cup. Once the mixture is cool enough to handle, pour to fill each mini-watermelon shell up to the edge. Once the top of the jello has set, transfer the filled mini-watermelon shells to a baking sheet and refrigerate for two hours or so.

6 Cut as desired. Sprinkle on some sea salt and serve.

## Ingredients

(Makes four jello-filled slices of pineapple)

- 4 pineapple slices cut width-wise [$\frac{3}{4}$" (2 cm) thickness]
- $\frac{3}{4}$ cup plus 4 teaspoons (200 ml) white wine (sweet white wine or soda)
- $\frac{3}{4}$ cup plus 4 teaspoons (200 ml) water
- $\frac{1}{3}$ cup plus 5 teaspoons (80 g) granulated sugar
- $2\frac{1}{2}$ tablespoons (20 g) agar

\<Fruits>

- Pineapple flesh as desired [dice into $\frac{1}{2}$" (1 cm) cubes]
- Kiwi 8 slices (peeled)
- Kiwi as desired [dice into $\frac{1}{2}$" (1 cm) cubes]

## Preparation

Slice pineapple. Leave $\frac{3}{4}$" (2 cm) from the peel and remove the flesh. Dice the flesh into $\frac{1}{2}$" (1 cm) cubes.

## Instructions

1  Place the pineapple slices on a baking sheet lined with plastic wrap. Put diced fruit inside the pineapple slices.

2  Combine granulated sugar and agar in a small bowl.

3  Pour white wine and water in a small saucepan. Add the sugar and agar mixture to the saucepan and whisk until dissolved.

4  Bring to a boil over medium heat. Once boiling, remove saucepan from heat. Pour mixture through a sieve into a measuring cup. Allow to cool.

5  Once the mixture is cool enough to handle, pour it into the pineapple slices prepared in step 1. Refrigerate for about an hour to set.

## TIPS

Once the mixture has cooled, be sure to quickly pour it into the pineapple slices as it is prone to setting up. To transfer the jello to a dish, place it on a plate without removing the plastic wrap then slide the plastic wrap out.

# Tropical Pineapple Jello

White Wine Jello with Papaya and Mango p.36

# White Wine Jello with Papaya and Mango

## Ingredients

(Makes four halved papaya shell jello cups)

- 4 papayas
- 40 pieces of papaya flesh
  (balled using a melon-baller)
- 4 tablespoons lemon juice

<Mango Jello>
- $^2/_3$ cup (160 ml) mango puree
- $^2/_3$ cup (160 ml) coconut cream
- 2 tablespoons plus 2 teaspoons
  (40 ml) milk
- $^1/_4$ cup plus $^1/_2$ teaspoon (50 g)
  granulated sugar
- 2 tablespoons condensed milk
- 6 g leaf gelatin

<White Wine Jello>
- $^3/_4$ cup plus 4 teaspoons (200 ml) white
  wine
  (can be substituted with soda)
- $^3/_4$ cup plus 4 teaspoons (200 ml) water
- $^1/_3$ cup (60 g) granulated sugar
- $2^1/_2$ tablespoons (20 g) agar

## Preparation

Halve each papaya lengthwise and remove the seeds.

Leave $^1/_2$" (1 cm) from the skin and scoop out the flesh.

Pour some lemon juice over the flesh and refrigerate.
Slice off the bottom of each hollowed papaya to create a stable platform (see photo).

Soak the leaf gelatin in cold water.

## Instructions

1  Prepare mango jello. Combine coconut cream, milk, granulated sugar, and condensed milk in a small saucepan. Heat on medium. Just before the mixture comes to a boil, add the leaf gelatin (remove any excess moisture) and whisk well until the gelatin dissolves. After the gelatin has dissolved, add mango puree and remove the saucepan from the heat. Put the bottom of the saucepan in a bowl filled with ice water to cool. After the mixture has thickened slightly, pour it in the papaya shells, filling to about 80%. Transfer the papaya shells to a baking sheet and refrigerate.

2  Prepare white wine jello. Combine granulated sugar and agar in a small bowl. Pour white wine and water into a small saucepan. Gradually add the sugar and agar mixture to the saucepan and whisk until dissolved. Bring to a boil over medium heat. Once boiling, remove saucepan from heat. Transfer the mixture to an airtight container and allow to cool. Then, refrigerate until the gelatin has completely set.

3  Just before serving, take the gelatin filled mango shells out of the refrigerator. Add some of the balled mango flesh to the top of each. Use a spoon to take up some white wine flavored gelatin and drop it over the balled mango flesh.

## TIPS

If you prefer to enjoy the distinct aroma of the papaya flesh, you can omit the lemon juice.

# Passion Fruit Coconut Jello

## Ingredients

(Makes sixteen halved passion fruit shell jello cups)

- 8 passion fruits
- $2/3$ cup (150 g) flesh
- $1 2/3$ cups (400 ml) water
- $1/3$ cup (60 g) granulated sugar
- 4 teaspoons (12 g) agar
- 4 tablespoons coconut syrup
- Yogurt, optional

## Preparation

Halve each passion fruit and remove the flesh. This will provide the flesh called for in the recipe.

## Instructions

1 Wrinkle up a sheet of plastic wrap and then lay it on either a muffin tin or a baking sheet. Then, add the hollowed passion fruit (see photo).

2 Combine granulated sugar and agar in a small bowl.

3 Pour water into a small saucepan. Gradually, add the sugar and agar mixture and whisk until dissolved.

4 Bring to a boil over medium heat. Once boiling, remove saucepan from heat. Pour mixture through a sieve into a measuring cup. Allow to cool.

5 Once the mixture has cooled, fill each passion fruit shell. Once the top of the jello has set, refrigerate for an hour or so.

6 If you desire, serve with a dollop of yogurt.

### TIPS

Lining a muffin tin with a sheet of plastic wrap helps to stabilize small sized fruits, like passion fruits.
Serving with whipped cream, instead of yogurt, is also quite delicious.

# Avocado and Banana Chia Seed Jello

## Ingredients

(Makes eight halved avocado shell jello cups)

- 4 avocados, whole flesh
- 4 tablespoons lemon juice
- 2 bananas
- 2 tablespoons chia seeds
- 1 2/3 cups (400 ml) water
- 2 1/2 tablespoons (30 g) granulated sugar
- 2 teaspoons (6 g) agar
- 2 tablespoons coconut syrup
- Maple syrup, optional

## Preparation

Slice through the avocado until you feel the knife hit the pit. Cut all the way around the pit. Twist the two halves apart. Scoop the flesh out using a spoon or melon-baller. Then, dice the flesh into bite-sized cubes.

Pour lemon juice over the flesh and the hollowed avocado shells to prevent oxidation.

Place the hollowed avocados on a muffin tin or a baking sheet lined with wrinkled plastic wrap. Set the flesh and the hollowed avocados aside in the refrigerator.

Soak chia seeds in 6 tablespoons of water (not included in the recipe) to soften.

## Instructions

1  Combine granulated sugar and agar in a small bowl.

2  Pour water into a small saucepan. Add the sugar and agar mixture and whisk until dissolved.

3  Bring to a boil over medium heat. Once boiling, add softened chia seeds. Bring to a boil again. Once boiling, remove saucepan from heat. Add coconut syrup and stir.

4  Once the mixture has cooled, transfer to an airtight container and refrigerate for about an hour to set.

5  Put diced avocado flesh and slices of banana inside each, refrigerated avocado shell. Then, top with the chia seed jello (in step 4).

6  If you desire, drizzle maple syrup over the shells and serve.

# Avocado Frozen Jello

**Ingredients** (Makes eight halved avocado shell jello cups)
- 4 avocados, whole flesh
- 2 tablespoons lemon juice
- 2 teaspoons (6 g) gelatin powder
- 4 tablespoons shredded coconut

[A]
- 4 tablespoons lemon juice
- 4 tablespoons lime juice
- 4 tablespoons honey
- 2 tablespoons coconut syrup

## Preparation

Slice through the avocado until you feel the knife hit the pit. Cut all the way around the pit. Twist the two halves apart.

Scoop the flesh out using a spoon or melon-baller. Then, dice the flesh into bite-sized cubes. Pour lemon juice over each hollowed avocado shell to prevent oxidization.

Place the hollowed avocados in a muffin tin or a baking sheet lined with wrinkled plastic wrap. Set them aside in the refrigerator.

Soak the gelatin powder in 4 tablespoons of water (not included in the recipe) to soften.

## Instructions

1  Put the avocado flesh and [A] into a food processor. Pulse to make puree.

2  Microwave (600 W) the softened gelatin powder for a minute. Then, add it to the puree and stir.

3  Fill each refrigerated avocado with the puree. Smooth the top using a spatula.

4  Freeze for over three hours.

5  Once the filling has frozen, cut as desired. Sprinkle on some shredded coconut and serve.

# Red Wine Vinegar Fig Jello

## Ingredients

(Makes eight fig shell jello cups)

- 8 figs
- ¾ cup (200 ml) red wine
- 2 tablespoons red wine vinegar
- 3 tablespoons plus 1 teaspoon (40 g) granulated sugar
- 1 tablespoon (8 g) agar
- Sour cream as desired

<Jam Sauce>
- ⅔ cup (100 g) fig flesh
- 6 tablespoons water
- 4 tablespoons granulated sugar
- 4 tablespoons red wine vinegar
- 1 tablespoon balsamic vinegar (optional)

## Preparation

Trim off the fig stems. Use a spoon or small melon-baller to remove the flesh. This will prepare the flesh called for in the recipe.

## Instructions

1 Wrinkle up plastic wrap and then lay it on a baking sheet. Place each hollowed fig on the baking sheet, on top of the wrinkled plastic wrap.

2 Combine granulated sugar and agar in a small bowl.

3 Add red wine and red wine vinegar to a small saucepan. Gradually, add the sugar and agar mixture to the saucepan. Whisk until dissolved. Bring to a boil over medium heat. Once boiling, remove saucepan from heat. Pour mixture into a measuring cup through a sieve and allow to cool. Once the mixture is cool enough to handle, pour it into the hollowed figs until each fig is filled (see picture). Once the top of the jello has set, refrigerate for an hour.

4 Prepare jam sauce. Add all of the ingredients to a saucepan and heat on medium. Use a spatula to mash the fig flesh and stir in the jam sauce mixture. Remove from the heat once the fig flesh has cooked down and reached a jam-like consistency. Allow to cool. Transfer the sauce to an airtight container and refrigerate.

5 Once the jello has set, cut figs as desired and place on a dish. Serve with the jam sauce and sour cream.

# Pomegranate Jello

## Ingredients

(Makes four halved pomegranate shell jello cups)

- 2 pomegranates
- 2 tablespoons pomegranate arils (i.e. seed pods)
- $1/3$ cup plus 4 teaspoons (100 ml) juice
- $1^1/4$ cups (300 ml) water
- $1/3$ cup (80 ml) pomegranate vinegar
- $2^1/2$ tablespoons (30 g) granulated sugar
- 2 tablespoons (16 g) agar

## Preparation

Begin cutting the pomegranate from the top (see photo A), then halve it (see photo B). Scoop out the arils using a spoon.

Set 2 tablespoons of arils aside. Transfer the remaining arils to a sieve and then mash them to prepare the juice called for in the recipe (see photo C).

## Instructions

1 Wrinkle up a sheet of plastic wrap and lay it on a baking sheet. Place each hollowed pomegranate on the baking sheet.

2 Combine granulated sugar and agar in a small bowl.

3 Pour water and pomegranate vinegar into a small saucepan. Add the sugar and agar mixture. Whisk until dissolved.

4 Bring to a boil over medium heat. Once boiling, add the juice to the mixture. Bring to a boil again. Once boiling, remove saucepan from heat. Pour mixture through a sieve into a measuring cup. Allow to cool.

5 Once the mixture is cool enough to handle, fill each pomegranate.

6 Once the top of the jello has set, refrigerate for an hour or so. Cut as desired and serve.

# Green Grape Balsamic Vinegar Jello

## Ingredients

(Makes thirty green grape jello cups)

- 30 green grapes
- $1/3$ cup plus 4 teaspoons (100 ml) water
- 2 tablespoons balsamic vinegar
- 2 tablespoons honey
- $1/2$ tablespoon (4 g) agar

## Preparation

Trim off the top of each grape (about a quarter of the grape). Also, trim off the bottom to make a stable platform out of the grape.

Scoop out about half of the flesh using a spoon or melon-baller (see photo). Transfer each grape to a baking sheet (enjoy the removed flesh as you wish as it is not required in the recipe).

## Instructions

1 Combine water, balsamic vinegar, and honey in a small saucepan. Add agar gradually and whisk well to dissolve.

2 Bring to a boil over medium heat. Once boiling, remove saucepan from heat. Pour mixture through a sieve into a measuring cup. Allow to cool.

3 Once the mixture is cool enough to handle, fill each hollowed grape. Once the top of the jello has set, refrigerate for an hour.

# Kyoho Grape Brandy Jello

## Ingredients

(Makes thirty Kyoho grape jello cups)

- 30 Kyoho grapes
- $1/3$ cup (80 ml) water
- 3 tablespoons plus 1 teaspoon (50 ml) brandy
- 2 tablespoons honey
- $1/2$ tablespoon (4 g) agar

## Preparation

Trim off the top of each Kyoho grape (about a quarter of the grape). Also, trim off the bottom to make a stable platform out of the grape.

Scoop out about a half of the flesh using a spoon or melon-baller (see photo). Transfer each grape to a baking sheet (enjoy the removed flesh as desired since it is not required in the recipe).

## Instructions

1 Combine water, brandy, and honey in a small saucepan. Add the agar gradually and whisk well to dissolve.

2 Bring to a boil over medium heat. Once boiling, remove saucepan from heat. Pour mixture through a sieve into a measuring cup. Allow to cool.

3 Once the mixture is cool enough to handle, fill each Kyoho grape. Once the top of the jello has set, refrigerate for an hour.

## Ingredients

(Makes twelve halved pear shell jello cups)

- 6 pears
- 2 cups plus 1⅓ tablespoons (500 ml) milk
- 2 tablespoons plus 2 teaspoons (40 ml) water
- ⅓ cup plus 1 tablespoon (80 g) granulated sugar
- 4 teaspoons (12 g) agar
- 4 tablespoons condensed milk

<Caramel Sauce>

- ⅓ cup (60 g) granulated sugar
- 2 tablespoons water
- 2 tablespoons hot water

## Preparation

Halve each pear lengthwise. Use a spoon or melon-baller to scoop out the core in a 1½" (4 cm) diameter circle.

## Instructions

1 Place the hollowed pears on a muffin tin or baking sheet lined with wrinkled plastic wrap.

2 Add granulated sugar and water to a small saucepan. Heat on medium. Swirl the saucepan until the mixture turns a light amber color. Then, slowly add half of the milk. Once the milk is incorporated uniformly, remove saucepan from heat.

3 Add the agar little-by-little to the remaining milk and whisk well to dissolve. Add mixture to the saucepan.

4 Once again set the saucepan over medium heat to bring to a boil. Add condensed milk and stir well.

5 Remove saucepan from heat. Pour mixture into a measuring cup through a sieve and let cool. Once the mixture is cool enough to handle, pour it into the cored pears. Once the top of the jello has set, refrigerate for an hour.

6 Prepare caramel sauce. Combine granulated sugar and water in a small saucepan. Heat on medium. When the mixture turns amber, swirl the saucepan until the mixture becomes uniformly colored. Once amber, remove from heat. Add hot water and swirl saucepan to stir. Transfer caramel sauce to a heat-resistant container.

7 Once the jello has set, cut as desired. Drizzle on some caramel sauce to serve.

## TIPS

To make the caramel sauce, stir the ingredients by swirling the saucepan.

# Pear Jello with Caramel Sauce

# Mandarin Orange Jello

## Ingredients

(Makes twelve halved mandarin orange shell jello cups)

- 10 mandarin oranges
- Flesh of 4 mandarin oranges
- 1²/₃ cups (400 ml) juice
- ³/₄ cup plus 4 teaspoons (200 ml) orange soda
- ¹/₃ cup (60 g) granulated sugar
- 1 tablespoon (8 g) agar

## Preparation

Halve the six mandarin oranges crosswise. Remove all the segments (see photo). Juice the segments to prepare the juice called in for the recipe.

For the remaining four mandarin oranges, peel and remove the flesh from each segment.

## Instructions

1 Place the hollowed oranges in a muffin tin or a baking sheet lined with wrinkled plastic wrap.

2 Put the flesh inside each hollowed orange as you flake them.

3 Combine granulated sugar and agar in a small bowl.

4 Pour half of the juice and orange soda into a small saucepan. Then, add the mixture gradually and whisk until dissolved.

5 Bring to a boil over medium heat. Once boiling, add remaining juice and stir. Bring to a boil again. Once boiling, remove saucepan from heat. Pour mixture through a sieve into a measuring cup. Allow to cool.

6 Once the mixture is cool enough to handle, fill each hollowed mandarin. Once the top of the jello has set, refrigerate for an hour or so. Cut as desired and serve.

A

B

# Winter Cherry Jasmine Tea Jello

## Ingredients

(Makes twenty winter cherry jello)

- 20 winter cherries (edible)
- 1²/₃ cups (400 ml) jasmine tea
- ¹/₄ cup plus ¹/₂ teaspoon (50 g) granulated sugar
- 2¹/₂ tablespoons (20 g) agar

## TIPS

Use winter cherries whose outer skins do not have tears.  Most winter cherries available early in the fall are large and have tough outer skins.

## Instructions

1 Tear off the very tip of the winter cherry's outer skin (see photo A) and place on a muffin tin or baking sheet lined with wrinkled plastic wrap.

2 Combine granulated sugar and agar in a small bowl.

3 Pour jasmine tea into a small saucepan. Add the sugar and agar mixture and whisk until dissolved.

4 Bring to a boil on medium. Once boiling, remove saucepan from heat. Pour mixture through a sieve into a measuring cup. Allow to cool.

5 Once the mixture is cool enough to handle, pour it from the opening at the very tip of the outer skin of each winter cherry and fill inside (see photo B).

6 Refrigerate for an hour or so until the jello sets.

# Apple Spice Tea Jello

## Ingredients
(Makes six halved apple shell jello cups)

- 3 apples
- 3 tablespoons plus 1 teaspoon (40 g) granulated sugar
- 2 tablespoons (16 g) agar

\<Apple Spice Tea\>

- 1¾ cups plus 4 teaspoons (440 ml) water
- 2 tablespoons of loose tea leaves of your choice
- Whole flesh of 3 apples
- 2 cinnamon sticks (broken in half)
- 6 cloves
- 3 tablespoons plus 1 teaspoon (40 g) granulated sugar

## TIPS
Steep the tea to bring out the tea and spice aroma.

## Preparation
Halve each apple lengthwise. ½ " (1 cm) inside from the skin, scoop out the flesh using a spoon or melon-baller.

Soak the hollowed apples in salt water (not included in the recipe) to prevent discoloration due to oxidization.

## Instructions

1 Place the hollowed apples on a muffin tin or a baking sheet lined with wrinkled plastic wrap.

2 Combine granulated sugar and agar in a small bowl.

3 Prepare apple spice tea. Pour water into a small saucepan and heat on medium. When the water has come to a boil, add the remaining ingredients of the apple spice tea and bring to a boil again. Remove the saucepan from heat and cover. Steep for five minutes. Then, transfer the tea to a container through a sieve.

4 Put the tea back into the small saucepan and slowly add the sugar and agar mixture. Whisk well until dissolved.

5 Bring to a boil on medium heat. Once boiling, remove saucepan from heat. Pour mixture through a sieve into a measuring cup. Allow to cool.

6 Once the mixture is cool enough to handle, fill each cored apple.

7 Once the top of the jello has set, refrigerate for an hour or so. Cut as desired and serve.

# Kumquat Earl Grey Milk Tea Jello

## Ingredients

(Makes thirty to forty kumquat jello cups)

- 30 to 40 kumquats, whole flesh
- ½ cup plus 1 teaspoon (100 g) granulated sugar
- 1¼ tablespoons (10 g) agar
- Condensed milk as desired

&lt;Milk Tea&gt;

- 1⅔ cups (400 ml) water
- ¾ cup plus 4 teaspoons (200 ml) milk
- 4 tablespoons Earl Grey tea, loose leaves
- 4 cardamom seeds

## Preparation

Trim off the stem of each kumquat ¼" (0.5 cm) below the stem. Also, slice off the bottom of each kumquat to create a stable platform.

Use a grapefruit knife to scoop out the flesh and set the kumquats aside on a baking sheet.

## Instructions

1 Combine granulated sugar and agar in a small bowl.

2 Prepare milk tea. Pour water into a small saucepan and bring to a boil over medium heat. Add loose Earl Grey tea leaves and cardamom seeds. Boil for a couple of minutes. Add milk and bring to a boil again. Remove saucepan from heat and cover. Steep for five minutes. Pour the tea through a sieve into a bowl.

3 Pour the tea back into the small saucepan. Gradually add the sugar and agar mixture. Whisk well to dissolve.

4 Bring tea to a boil on medium heat. Pour mixture through a sieve into a measuring cup. Allow to cool.

5 Once the mixture is cool enough to handle, fill each kumquat.

6 Refrigerate for over an hour. Drizzle condensed milk over to serve.

## TIPS

Steep the tea to bring out the Earl Grey tea and spice aroma.

# Yuzu *Wagashi* Jello

## Ingredients
(Makes eight halved *yuzu* shell jello cups)
- 6 yuzu

**<*Shiro-An* Jello>**
- 4 teaspoons juice
- ½ teaspoon yuzu zest
- ½ cup (200 g) *shiro-an* (white bean paste)
- ¾ cup plus 4 teaspoons (200 ml) water
- 3 tablespoons plus 1 teaspoon (40 g) granulated sugar
- 2 tablespoons (8 g) agar

**<*Yuzu* Jello>**
- 2 tablespoons juice
- ½ teaspoon yuzu zest
- 1¼ cups (300 ml) water
- ⅓ cup (60 g) granulated sugar
- 2 tablespoons (16 g) agar

## Preparation
Halve four yuzu lengthwise. Remove the flesh as well as all remaining inner membranes.

Squeeze the flesh for the juice required by the recipe. Grate two of the remaining yuzu for the zest required by the recipe.

## Instructions
1 Place hollowed yuzu on a muffin tin or a baking sheet lined with wrinkled plastic wrap.

2 Prepare *shiro-an* jello. Combine granulated sugar and agar in a small bowl. Combine juice, *shiro-an*, and water in a small saucepan. Gradually add the sugar and agar mixture to the saucepan as you stir. Bring to a boil over medium heat. Once boiling, remove saucepan from heat. Pour mixture through a sieve into a measuring cup. Once the mixture is cool enough to handle, fill each hollowed yuzu half way. Once the top of the jello has set, refrigerate for about twenty minutes.

3 Prepare yuzu jello. Combine granulated sugar and agar in a small bowl. Pour juice and water into a small saucepan. Gradually add the sugar and agar mixture to the saucepan and whisk until dissolved. Bring to a boil over medium heat. Once boiling, remove from heat. Pour mixture through a sieve into a measuring cup. Once the mixture is cool enough to handle, pour it into each hollowed yuzu. Fill to the edge.

4 Once the top of the jello has set, refrigerate for an hour or so. Cut as desired and serve.

**TIPS**
Pour the second mixture after the previous layer has completely set in order to make beautiful layers.

# | APPETIZERS |

Jello can make fun appetizers.
Consommé, broth, wine-based jello, vegetables with
delightful textures and colors wrapped around pâté,
or cheese—all form light, delicious side-dishes that
make the perfect accompaniment for your drinks.

# White Turnip Seafood Jello

**Ingredients** (Makes eight white turnip shell jello cups)
- 8 white turnips
- 1⅔ cups (400 ml) water
- 4 tablespoons *shirodashi* (white soy sauce with broth)
- 4 tablespoons *sake*
- ½ teaspoon yuzu pepper seasoning
- 6 g leaf gelatin
- 4 tablespoons flying fish roe
- 4 tablespoons salmon roe
- 2 scallops

## Preparation

Wash the turnips. Lop off the stems about ½" (1 cm) below their base. Also, slice off the bottom of each turnip to create a stable platform.

Place the white turnips in a microwave-safe dish and microwave (600 W), while covered, for about three to four minutes until they become soft.

Use a grapefruit knife or spoon to hollow out each turnip leaving a gap ½" (1 cm) in from the skin. Place each hollowed turnip on a baking sheet and refrigerate (the portions that were removed aren't used in the recipe so use them as you wish).

Soak the leaf gelatin in cold water.

## Instructions

1 Pour water, *shirodashi*, *sake*, and yuzu pepper seasoning into a small saucepan. Heat on medium.

2 After bringing to a boil, remove from heat. Remove moisture from the leaf gelatin and then add to the saucepan. Whisk until gelatin is dissolved.

3 Place the bottom of the saucepan in a bowl filled with ice water to cool.

4 Once the gelatin mixture is cool and has thickened, add flying fish roe and stir. Transfer the mixture to an airtight container and refrigerate for an hour or so.

5 Quarter the scallops and distribute them inside each hollowed out, refrigerated, white turnip. Mush the jello and spoon out over the scallops filling the white turnip. Garnish with some salmon roe and serve.

## TIPS

Adjust cooking time according to turnip size.

# Broad Beans Jello

### Ingredients

(Makes sixteen halved broad bean pod jello cups)

- 20 broad bean pods
- 1²⁄₃ cups (400 ml) water
- 4 tablespoons *shirodashi* (white soy sauce with broth)
- 2 tablespoons (16 g) agar
- Black pepper (optional)

### Preparation

Halve pods and remove beans. Remove the inner membrane of each halved pod with a spoon and place on a baking sheet.

Boil the broad beans for three minutes and then drain. Blanch to cool and remove skin.

### Instructions

1  Place the shelled broad beans on each halved pod on the baking sheet.

2  Pour water and *shirodashi* into a small saucepan. Gradually add agar and whisk until dissolved.

3  Bring to a boil over medium heat. Once boiling, remove from heat. Pour mixture through a sieve into a measuring cup. Allow to cool.

4  Once the mixture has cooled, fill each halved pod. Once the top of the jello has set, refrigerate for an hour or so.

5  Transfer the broad bean jello to a serving dish. If you prefer, sprinkle some coarsely milled black pepper over everything and serve.

### TIPS

Be careful not to overcook the broad beans as they tend to cook quite quickly.

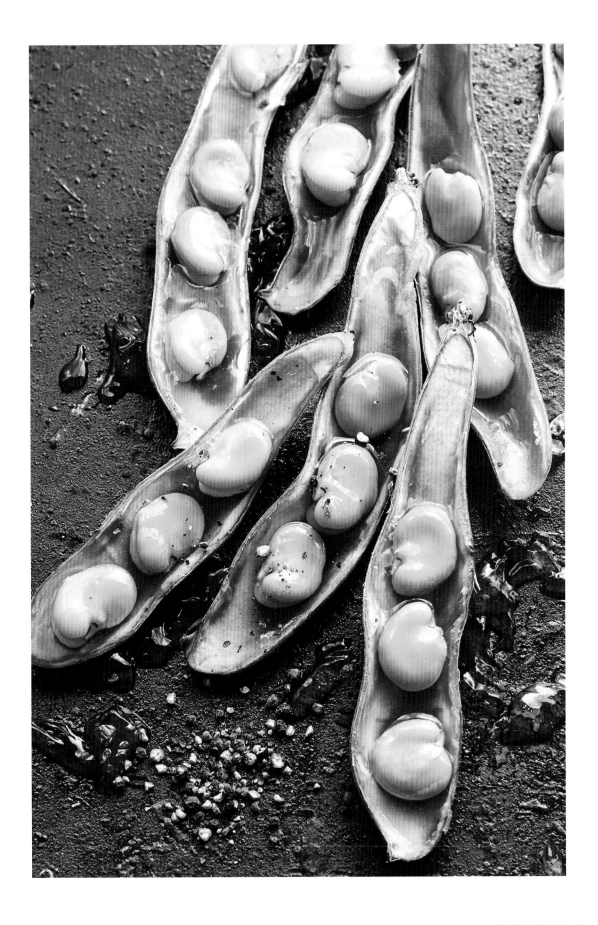

BROAD BEANS | 71

# Wine Jello Chicory with Pâté

**Ingredients** (Makes twenty-four chicory leaf jello cups)
- 24 leaves of chicory (including green and red)
- $2/3$ cup (160 ml) white wine
- 2 tablespoons plus 2 teaspoons (40 ml) red wine
- 1 teaspoon granulated sugar
- 2 teaspoons (6 g) agar
- Thyme as desired
- Sea salt as desired

\<Filling\>
- $1/4$ cup (40 g) Pâté de Campagne
  [dice into $1/4$" (0.5 cm) cubes]
- 8 pickled cucumbers
  [dice into $1/4$" (0.5 cm) cubes]

**Preparation**

Separate each chicory leaf from its core. Soak in cold water to make crisp. Then, dry the leaves using a kitchen towel or some paper towel.

Wrinkle up a sheet of plastic wrap and line a baking sheet. Place all the chicory leaves on the baking sheet and set aside.

**Instructions**

1 Place filling in the indentations on each chicory leaf.

2 Combine granulated sugar and agar in a small bowl.

3 Pour white wine and red wine into a small saucepan. Add the sugar and agar mixture and whisk until dissolved.

4 Bring to a boil over medium heat. Once boiling, remove from the heat. Pour mixture through a sieve into a measuring cup. Allow to cool. Once the mixture is cool enough to handle, fill each chicory leaf. Once the top of the jello has set, refrigerate for an hour.

5 Transfer the jello to a serving dish. Garnish with thyme and sea salt to serve.

# Onion and Red Cabbage Jello

## Ingredients

(Makes eight halved onion jello cups)

- 2 white onions and 2 red onions (medium sized)
- $1/3$ cup plus 4 teaspoons (100 ml) water
- 2 teaspoons (6 g) agar
- Parmesan cheese as desired

[A]
- 1 tablespoon finely chopped onion
- $1/3$ cup (30 g) red cabbage [dice into $3/4$" (2 cm) cubes]
- $3/4$ cup plus 4 teaspoons (200 ml) water
- 1 tablespoon vegetable bouillon (powder)
- 1 tablespoon vinegar
- A pinch of salt

## Preparation

Peel the skin and cut off the top and bottom of each onion (see photo A). Halve each onion crosswise.

Remove the inner layers up to $1/2$" (1 cm) from the outer edge. Push the layers for easier removal.

Cut the removed layers in half crosswise (see photo B). To make an onion container, put the bottom half of the removed layer in the halved onion (see photo C).

Place the onion containers in a microwave-safe dish and microwave (600 W), while covered, for about four minutes. Allow to cool.

Finely chop leftover onions to prepare the chopped onion called for in the recipe.

## Instructions

1 Transfer onion container to a baking sheet.

2 Add [A] to a small saucepan and heat on medium until the onions become transparent.

3 Add water and agar to a bowl. Whisk well until dissolved.

4 Add the agar mixture to the small saucepan and bring to a boil. Once boiling, remove saucepan from heat and allow to cool.

5 Once the mixture is cool enough to handle, fill each onion container.

6 Once the top of the jello has set, refrigerate for an hour or so. Serve with grated Parmesan cheese.

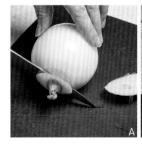

# Tomato Jello with Mozzarella Cheese

**Ingredients** (Makes twenty cherry tomato jello cups)

- 20 cherry tomatoes
- ³⁄₄ cup plus 4 teaspoons (200 ml) tomato juice
- ¹⁄₃ cup plus 4 teaspoons (100 ml) white wine
- A pinch of salt
- 2 teaspoons (6 g) agar
- 2 tablespoons lemon juice
- 20 bocconcini
- 40 capers
- Basil as desired
- Olive oil as desired

## Preparation

Trim off cherry tomato stems. Use a spoon or melon-baller to remove seeds and cores.

Strain the removed seeds and core to prepare the tomato juice called for in the recipe. Refrigerate all the trimmed stems.

## Instructions

1 Wrinkle up a sheet of plastic wrap and lay it on either a muffin tin or a baking sheet. Then, securely add each hollowed cherry tomato.

2 Add tomato juice, white wine, salt, and agar to a small saucepan. Whisk until dissolved. Then, heat the saucepan on medium and bring to a boil.

3 Once boiling, remove from heat. Add lemon juice and stir well. Pour mixture through a sieve into a measuring cup. Allow to cool.

4 Once the mixture is cool enough to handle, fill ³⁄₄ of each hollowed cherry tomato. Put bocconcini and some capers in each cherry tomato. Once the top of the jello has set, refrigerate for an hour.

5 Transfer tomato jello to a serving dish. Put the stems on top. Garnish with fresh basil leaves and drizzle some olive oil over everything to serve.

Watermelon Gazpacho Jello

**Ingredients** (Makes two mini watermelon jello cups)

- 2 mini watermelons [6" (15 cm) diameter]
- 1½ cups (600 ml) watermelon juice
- 4¼ tablespoons (34 g) agar
- 3 teaspoons salt

[A]

- 1¼ cups (200 g) watermelon flesh
- 1 cup (200 g) tomato (remove the skin and seeds)
- ½ clove garlic
- 2 tablespoons olive oil
- 4 teaspoons white wine vinegar
- 2 teaspoons sherry vinegar (optional)

A

[B]

- 40 pieces of balled watermelon flesh
- 4 tablespoons celery stalks [dice into ¼" (0.5 cm) cubes]
- 4 tablespoons cucumber [dice into ¼" (0.5 cm) cubes]
- 4 tablespoons lemon juice

B

**Preparation**

Lop off the top of the mini watermelon to create a flat, stable surface (see photo A).

Score a line 2" (5 cm) up from the bottom of the watermelon. Then, split the watermelon using your hand (see photo B).

Use a spoon or melon-baller to scoop out the flesh in a ball-shape (40 balls needed). Then refrigerate.

Further remove the flesh and set aside 1¼ cups (200 g). Put the remaining flesh in a sieve and mush using a spatula to prepare the juice called for in the recipe.

**Instructions**

1  Put ingredients [A] in a blender and mix together.

2  Add half of the watermelon juice to a small saucepan. Then, add agar little-by-little and whisk until dissolved.

3  Bring to a boil over medium heat. Once boiling, add the remaining watermelon juice and salt. Remove the saucepan from the heat before it boils. Let cool.

4  Once the mixture is cool enough to handle, add ingredients [B] and stir.

5  Place the hollowed mini watermelon on a baking sheet. Fill with mixture and refrigerate for an hour or so.

**TIPS**

Sherry vinegar adds a certain sourness, thus providing a refreshing taste.

# Smoked Salmon and Grapefruit Jello

## Ingredients

(Makes four halved grapefruit shell jello cups)

- 2 grapefruits
- 10 g leaf gelatin
- Coarsely chopped dill as desired
- Olive oil as desired

[A]
- 4 tablespoons grapefruit juice
- $\frac{3}{4}$ cup plus 4 teaspoons (200 ml) white wine
- $\frac{3}{4}$ cup plus 4 teaspoons (200 ml) water
- $\frac{2}{3}$ teaspoon salt

<Filling>
- 12 pieces of grapefruit flesh
- 8 slices of smoked salmon (cut in half)
- 40 small capers
- Coarsely chopped dill as desired

## Preparation

Halve each grapefruit lengthwise. Remove the flesh using a grapefruit knife. Remove all remaining inner membranes.

Set aside 12 sections of grapefruit flesh, remove the membrane, and halve the flesh. Juice remaining flesh to prepare the juice called for in the recipe.

Soak the leaf gelatin in cold water.

## Instructions

1 Place hollowed grapefruit in a muffin tin or a baking sheet lined with wrinkled plastic wrap.

2 Add each filling to the inside of the grapefruit in layers.

3 Add [A] to a small saucepan and heat on medium.

4 Once [A] has boiled, remove saucepan from heat. Take the leaf gelatin you soaked in cold water and remove any excess moisture. Then, add leaf gelatin to the small saucepan. Whisk well and make sure the gelatin dissolves.

5 Put the saucepan in a bowl filled with ice water to cool.

6 Once the gelatin becomes slightly thick, pour the mixture into each grapefruit.

7 Refrigerate for an hour or more to set the gelatin. Cut as desired. Garnish with coarsely chopped dill and drizzle on some olive oil.

## TIPS

Enjoy leftover grapefruit juice as you wish.

# Tri-Color Bell
# Pepper Jello

**Ingredients** (Makes twelve halved bell pepper shell jello cups)
- 2 red peppers, 2 yellow peppers, and 2 orange peppers
- 2½ cups (600 ml) water
- Half an onion (finely chopped)
- 4 bouillon cubes
- 3 tablespoons plus 2 teaspoons (30 g) agar
- 3 teaspoons salt

<Filling for the Red Peppers>
- 20 pieces of ham [dice into ¼" (0.5 cm) cubes]
- 12 pieces of cheese [dice into ¼" (0.5 cm) cubes]

<Filling for the Yellow Peppers>
- 6 tablespoons of cooked edamame (shelled)

<Filling for the Orange Peppers>
- Slices of 8 to 10 black olives (pitted)
- 2 teaspoons capers

## Preparation
Halve each pepper lengthwise. Do not trim off the stem, but do remove the seeds.

## Instructions
1 Place the peppers in a microwave-safe dish and microwave (600 W), while covered, for about forty to fifty seconds. Then, blanch them in a cold water.

2 Dry off the peppers with a tea towel. Place them on a baking sheet lined with wrinkled plastic warp. Then, add filling to the inside of each pepper.

3 Combine water, chopped onion, and bouillon cubes in a saucepan set over medium heat. Once the onion has become translucent, add salt to taste and remove saucepan from heat.

4 Add 4 tablespoons of water (not included in the recipe) to the agar and whisk well to dissolve. Add agar mixture to the saucepan and bring to a boil over medium heat. Once boiling, remove from heat.

5 Transfer the mixture to a measuring cup and let cool. Once cool enough to handle, fill each pepper up to the edge.

6 Once the top of the jello has set, refrigerate for an hour or so. Cut as desired and serve.

**TIPS**
The filling can be substituted with ingredients of your choice. Steamed chicken breast, tuna, corn, or boiled eggs also make delightful filling.

Round Zucchini Jello with Crab p.86

Zucchini Jello with Green Sauce p.87

# Round Zucchini Jello with Crab

## Ingredients
(Makes eight halved round zucchini shell jello cups)
- 4 round zucchinis [$3^{1}/_{8}$" (8 cm) diameter]
- $2^{1}/_{2}$ cups (600 ml) water
- 2 tablespoons vegetable bouillon (powder)
- $^{1}/_{2}$ tablespoon (4 g) *kanten* (Japanese agar) powder
- 4 teaspoons lemon juice

[A]
- $^{1}/_{8}$ cup plus 1 teaspoon (60 g) flaked crab meat
- $^{2}/_{3}$ cup (100 g) zucchini flesh (finely chopped)
- $^{3}/_{8}$ cup (40 g) celery (finely chopped)
- 1 tablespoon white wine
- 2 teaspoons salt

## Preparation
Halve each round zucchini lengthwise. Score a line $^{1}/_{4}$" (0.5 cm) in from the skin using a grapefruit knife.

Use a spoon or melon-baller to scoop out the flesh along the scored line and set aside.

Finely chop the flesh to prepare for that which is called for in the recipe.

## Instructions
1  Place the hollowed, round zucchinis on a baking sheet lined with wrinkled plastic wrap.

2  Combine water, vegetable bouillon powder, and *kanten* powder in a small saucepan and whisk well to dissolve. Bring to a boil over medium heat. Once boiling, reduce the heat to low and boil for a couple minutes.

3  Add [A] to the small saucepan and bring to a boil again. Once boiling, remove from heat and add lemon juice. Let cool.

4  Once the mixture is cool enough to handle, quickly fill each zucchini up to the edge.

5  Refrigerate for an hour or so. Cut as desired and serve.

## TIPS
Since the agar mixture will set quickly, pour it into each zucchini shell quickly.

**Ingredients** (For four zucchinis)

- 2 green and 2 yellow zucchinis
- 3⅓ cups (800 ml) water
- 2 tablespoons vegetable bouillon (powder)
- 4 tablespoons white wine
- 2 tablespoons white wine vinegar
- 5 tablespoons (40 g) agar
- 2 tablespoons lemon juice
- 2 teaspoons salt

\<Basil Sauce\>
- 20 basil leaves
- 6 tablespoons parsley (finely chopped)
- ¼ cup plus 2 tablespoons olive oil
- 2 tablespoons lemon juice
- 2 teaspoons salt

\<Basil Cheese Sauce\>
- 4 tablespoons zucchini flesh (pureed)
- 10 basil leaves
- 2 tablespoons parsley (finely chopped)
- 10 capers
- 4 tablespoons Parmesan cheese (grated)
- 4 tablespoons olive oil
- 2 tablespoons white wine vinegar
- 2 tablespoons lemon juice
- 1 teaspoon salt

**Preparation**

Cut each zucchini into ½" (1.5 cm) thick slices.
Push through a round cookie cutter (photo A) (use a knife if you don't have a round cookie cutter), while leaving ⅛" (0.3 cm) around the skin.

Cover and microwave (600 W) the zucchini slices for about two minutes. Then, pulse to prepare the puree required by the recipe.

**Instructions**

1 Place the hollowed zucchini slices in a microwave-safe dish and microwave (600 W), while covered, for about forty to fifty seconds. Then, blanch in cold water.

2 Dry off the hollowed zucchini slices with a tea towel. Then, transfer to a dish and refrigerate.

3 Combine water, vegetable bouillon powder, white wine, and white wine vinegar in a small saucepan. Add agar gradually to the saucepan and whisk well to dissolve.

4 Bring to a boil over medium heat. Once boiling, remove the saucepan from heat and add lemon juice and salt. Pour mixture through a sieve into a measuring cup. Allow to cool.

5 Once cool enough to handle, remove the hollowed zucchini slices from the refrigerator. Then, pour mixture into each slice. Fill to the edge (see photo B). Use a knife to smooth out the surface and remove any air bubbles (see photo C). Then, refrigerate for an hour or so.

6 Prepare the basil sauce and basil cheese sauce separately using a food processor. Then, refrigerate.

7 Once the jello has set, garnish with some basil leaves and serve with the basil and basil cheese sauce.

# Zucchini Jello with Green Sauce

**TIPS**

Since the agar mixture will set quickly, pour it into each zucchini slice quickly. The mixture should only be slightly thick. Prepare both sauces just before serving or discoloration will occur.

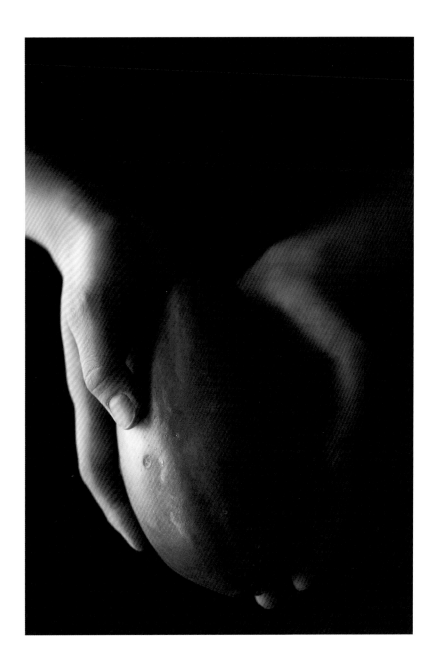

# Young Papaya Jello

## Ingredients

(Makes four halved green papaya shell jello cups)

- 2 green papayas [4¾" (12 cm) diameter]
- ¾ cup plus 4 teaspoons (200 ml) water
- 2 teaspoons fish sauce
- 1 teaspoon salt
- 1 tablespoon plus 2 teaspoons (14 g) agar
- Cilantro as desired
- Sweet chili sauce as desired

&lt;Filling&gt;
- 12 pieces small shelled shrimps
- Flesh of 2 papayas (julienned)
- 2 clove of garlic (grated)
- 2 tablespoons cilantro (finely chopped)
- 2 teaspoons salt
- 2 tablespoons lemon juice
- 2 tablespoons lime juice

## Preparation

Halve each papaya lengthwise and remove the seeds.

Use a grapefruit knife to score a line ¼" (0.5 cm) inside from the skin. Then, scoop out the flesh along the scored line using a spoon or melon-baller.

Julienne the flesh (use a mandolin slicer if you prefer).

## Instructions

1 Place the hollowed papayas on a baking sheet lined with wrinkled plastic wrap.

2 Cook the shelled shrimp in boiling water that has some added *sake* (not included in the recipe). Then, blanch in cold water.

3 Dry off the shrimp well. Combine all of the filling ingredients and the shrimp in a bowl. Then, put the filling in each hollowed papaya.

4 Combine water, fish sauce, and salt in a small saucepan. Then, add agar gradually to the small saucepan and whisk well to dissolve.

5 Bring to a boil over medium heat. Once boiling, remove saucepan from heat. Pour mixture through a sieve into a measuring cup. Allow to cool.

6 Once the mixture has cooled enough to handle, fill each papaya up to the edge. Once the top of the jello has set, refrigerate for an hour or so.

7 Once the jello has completely set, cut as desired. Serve with some cilantro and sweet chili sauce.

## TIPS

The agar mixture will set quickly, so pour it into each papaya as soon as it begins to thicken.

# Persimmon Jello with Camembert Cheese and Rum Raisins

---

## Ingredients

(Makes eight halved persimmon shell jello cups)

- 4 persimmons
- $2/3$ cup (160 ml) water
- 2 tablespoons plus 2 teaspoons (40 ml) white wine
- 2 tablespoons plus $2^{1}/2$ teaspoons (34 g) granulated sugar
- 1 tablespoon (8 g) agar

&lt;Filling&gt;

- 0.7 oz (20 g) Camembert cheese (dice into bite-sized cube)
- 20 rum raisins

## Preparation

Halve each persimmon and trim off the stems.

Score a line $1/2$" (1 cm) in from the skin using a grapefruit knife.

Use a spoon or melon-baller to scoop out the flesh along the scored line (enjoy the flesh as you wish since it is not required in the recipe).

## Instructions

1 Place the hollowed persimmons on a baking sheet lined with wrinkled plastic wrap.

2 Add filling to each persimmon.

3 Combine granulated sugar and agar in a small bowl.

4 Pour water and white wine into a small saucepan. Gradually add agar and whisk until dissolved.

5 Bring to a boil over medium heat. Once boiling, remove saucepan from heat. Pour mixture through a sieve into a measuring cup. Allow to cool.

6 Once cool enough to handle, fill each persimmon up to the edge.

7 Once the top of the jello has set, refrigerate for an hour or so. Cut as desired and serve.

# Beet Jello

**Ingredients** (Makes four halved beet shell jello cups)
- 2 beets [4" to 4¾" (10 to 12 cm) diameter]
- 1¼ cups (300 ml) milk
- 8 g leaf gelatin
- 1 teaspoon salt
- Heavy cream, optional

[A]
- 1⅓ cups (200 ml) flesh
- A quarter of an onion (finely chopped)
- 1¼ cups (300 ml) water
- 2 bouillon cubes

**Preparation**

Wash beets well. Halve and cook in plenty of hot water until very tender.

For each cooked beet, score a line ½" (1 cm) in from the skin using a grapefruit knife.

Scoop out the flesh along the scored line and set aside.

Soak leaf gelatin in cold water.

**Instructions**

1  Place the hollowed beet halves in a baking sheet lined with wrinkled plastic wrap. Set them aside in a refrigerator.

2  Combine all ingredients [A] in a small saucepan. Bring to a boil over medium heat. Once boiling, reduce the heat to low and cook until the onion becomes translucent.

3  Transfer the mixture to a food processor and pulse to puree.

4  Transfer the puree back to the small saucepan and add the milk and salt. Heat on medium. Just as it begins to boil, remove saucepan from the heat.

5  Remove excess moisture from leaf gelatin and then add to the saucepan. Stir well.

6  Put the bottom of the saucepan in a bowl filled with ice water to cool.

7  Once the mixture become slightly thick, pour it into each beet. Fill to the edge. Refrigerate for over an hour. If desired, serve with a dollop of heavy cream.

Author Profile

## Naomi Hakamata

Hakamata is a food stylist and food coordinator. She started her
career as a designer at an automobile company and then moved to the
west coast of the United States. The foods and lifestyle in California
provoked her to polish her visual sense and culinary skills, mainly
making desserts. After returning to Japan, she started "& N kitchen
studio." She now proposes ideas like, "The fusion of food and style" and
actively propagates her ideas through magazines and advertisements.
Her sophisticated food stylings are always well received. In pursuit of
new foods for life, she has been developing her own original recipes.
Her recent publications include: *Flower sweets: edible flower de tsukuru
romantic na otona sweets* (Seibundo Shinkosha)

Incredible Jello: Over 40 Fantastic Appetizers and Desserts
by Naomi Hakamata

Text, images and design copyright © 2018 Graphc-sha Publishing Co., Ltd.

First designed and published in Japan in 2018 by:
Graphic-sha Publishing Co., Ltd.

English edition published in 2019 by:
NIPPAN IPS Co., Ltd.
1-3-4 Yushima
Bunkyo-ku Tokyo,
113-0034 Japan

ISBN 978-4-86505-224-4

Printed in China

10 9 8 7 6 5 4 3 2 1

Original edition creative staff

| | |
|---|---|
| Book design: | Tetsuya Yuasa (colonbooks) |
| Photographs: | Teruaki Kawakami (bean) |
| Assistant to the photographer: | Haruna Uehashi (bean) |
| Assistant to cooking: | Ritsuko Aita, Emi Kagaya |
| Editor: | Yoko Koike (Graphics-sha Publishing Co., Ltd.) |

English edition

| | |
|---|---|
| English translation: | Kevin Wilson |
| English edition layout: | Shinichi Ishioka |
| Production and management: | Kumiko Sakamoto (Graphic-sha Publishing Co., Ltd.) |